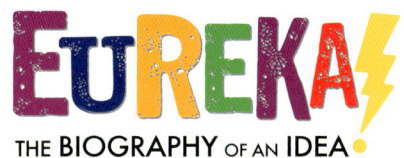

EUREKA!

THE BIOGRAPHY OF AN IDEA

VIDEO GAMES

BY CHERYL KIM • ILLUSTRATED BY OLGA LEE

KANEPRESS

AN IMPRINT OF ASTRA BOOKS FOR YOUNG READERS

New York

For Nathanael and Zachary—CK

To my dear nephews—OL

Special thanks to Kelsey Lewin, Co-Director,
The Video Game History Foundation

Astra Publishing House is not affiliated with or sponsored by any companies referenced in this book.

Library of Congress Cataloging-in-Publication Data

Names: Kim, Cheryl, author. | Lee, Olga, illustrator.
Title: Video games / by Cheryl Kim ; illustrated by Olga Lee.
Description: New York : Kane Press, an imprint of Astra Books for Young
    Readers, 2024. | Series: Eureka! the biography of an idea | Audience:
    Ages 4-8 | Audience: Grades K-1 | Summary: "Games have been around for
    thousands of years, but with the first blips on a screen, they really
    got electric. Now video games are better than ever, ready for on-the-go,
    great for sharing with friends, and even with immersive virtual reality.
    Video Games is an entertaining and informative look at the development
    of an invention that keeps kids of all ages entertained"—Provided by publisher.
Identifiers: LCCN 2023034749 | ISBN 9781662670534 (hardcover) |
    ISBN 9781662670114 (trade paperback) | ISBN 9781662670121 (ebk)
Subjects: LCSH: Video games—Juvenile literature.
Classification: LCC GV1469.3 .K543 2024 | DDC 794.8—dc23/eng/20230802
LC record available at https://lccn.loc.gov/2023034749

Kane Press
An imprint of Astra Books for Young Readers,
a division of Astra Publishing House
kanepress.com
Printed in Malaysia

10 9 8 7 6 5 4 3 2 1

BEFORE TVs, COMPUTERS, AND CELL PHONES, what did people do for fun? Just like now, they played games! Those games led to the video games we know today.

Are you ready? Hit PLAY and let's get STARTED.

The first known board game, senet, dates back over 5,000 years! In Egypt, players raced to move their tokens to the end of the board.

Other games popped up around the world. A dice game, snakes and ladders, from India.

Mancala, a stone moving game, from Africa.

Dominoes from China.

AMERICA, 1800s

In the late 1800s, Montague Redgrave used a spring to build a "ball shooter" game. This early version of a pinball machine put table-top games on the map.

AMERICA, EARLY 1900s

Across the United States, penny arcades sprang up. An **arcade** gathered lots of games in one place. By dropping a coin through a slot, players could try different machines.

Test your strength against a mechanical hand!
Roll a ball into a bull's-eye ring!
Grab a piece of candy with a crane and claw!
People had more game choices now than ever before.

But wait! Let's hit PAUSE.
Around this time along came a powerful force that
was the ultimate game changer—ELECTRICITY!

APOLLO

SKEE-BALL

GERMANY, 1897

First, electrical engineer Karl Ferdinand Braun came up with an important invention. He placed two metal plates and a special glass plate inside a glass tube. He pumped all the air out of the tube. Then he connected the metal plates to an electrical source.

A ray of light shot out from the metal plate through the tube. The other end glowed!

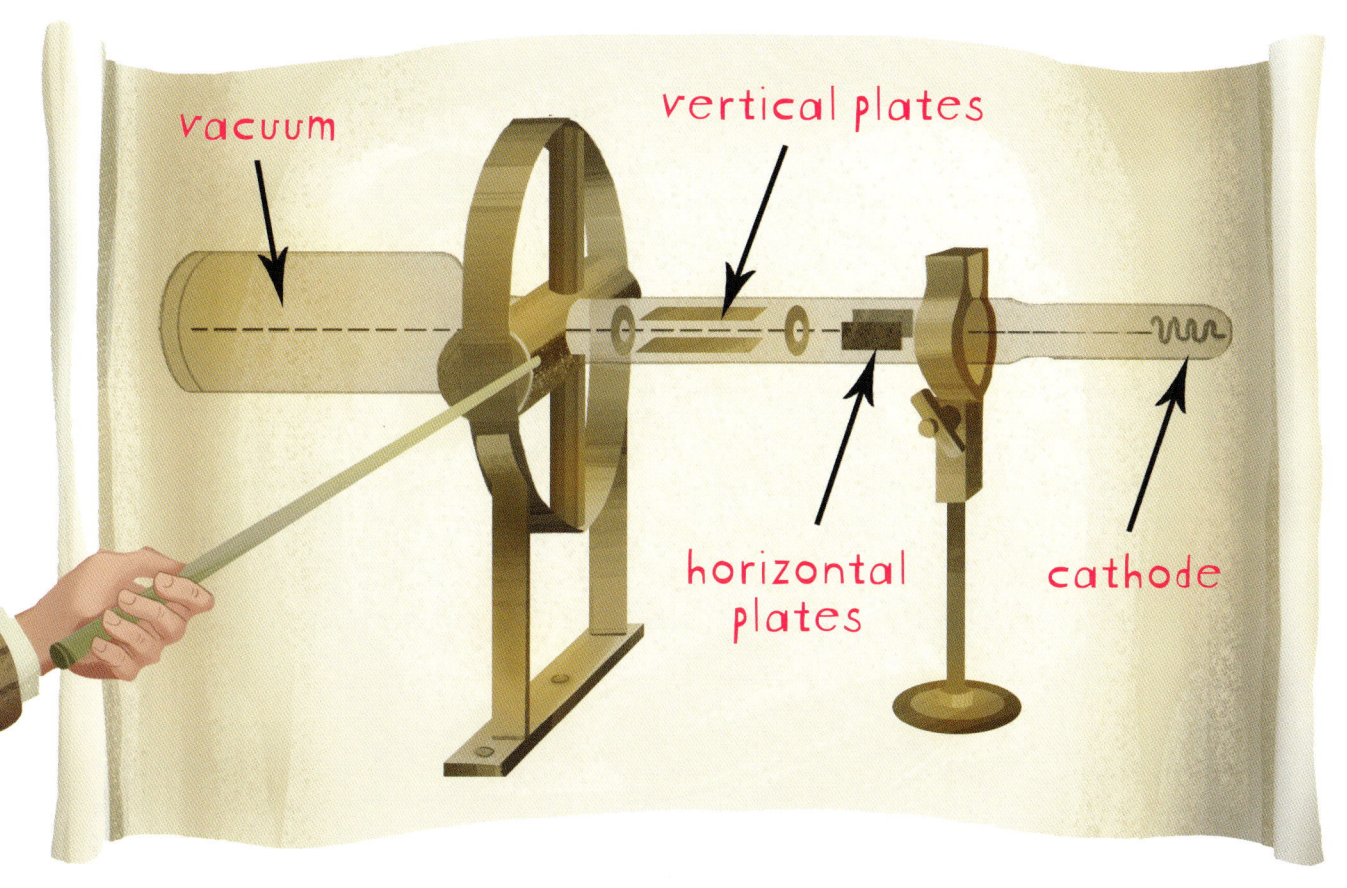

vacuum

vertical plates

horizontal plates

cathode

Braun had invented the first **cathode-ray tube**, or CRT. Over the next few decades, inventors used the CRT to project moving images. CRTs paved the way for TV and computer screens.

NEW YORK, 1958

William Higinbotham worked at a computer lab. Once a year, the lab opened to the public. Usually, visitors just stood back and looked. How could Higinbotham make it more exciting?

Thanks to CRTs, he designed a game called *Tennis for Two*. Each player held a metal controller. To hit the ball, they pressed a button. To control the angle of the ball, they turned a knob.

The lab guests loved his game! A very long line formed. Higinbotham's two-player computer game was the first made for fun, not just research.

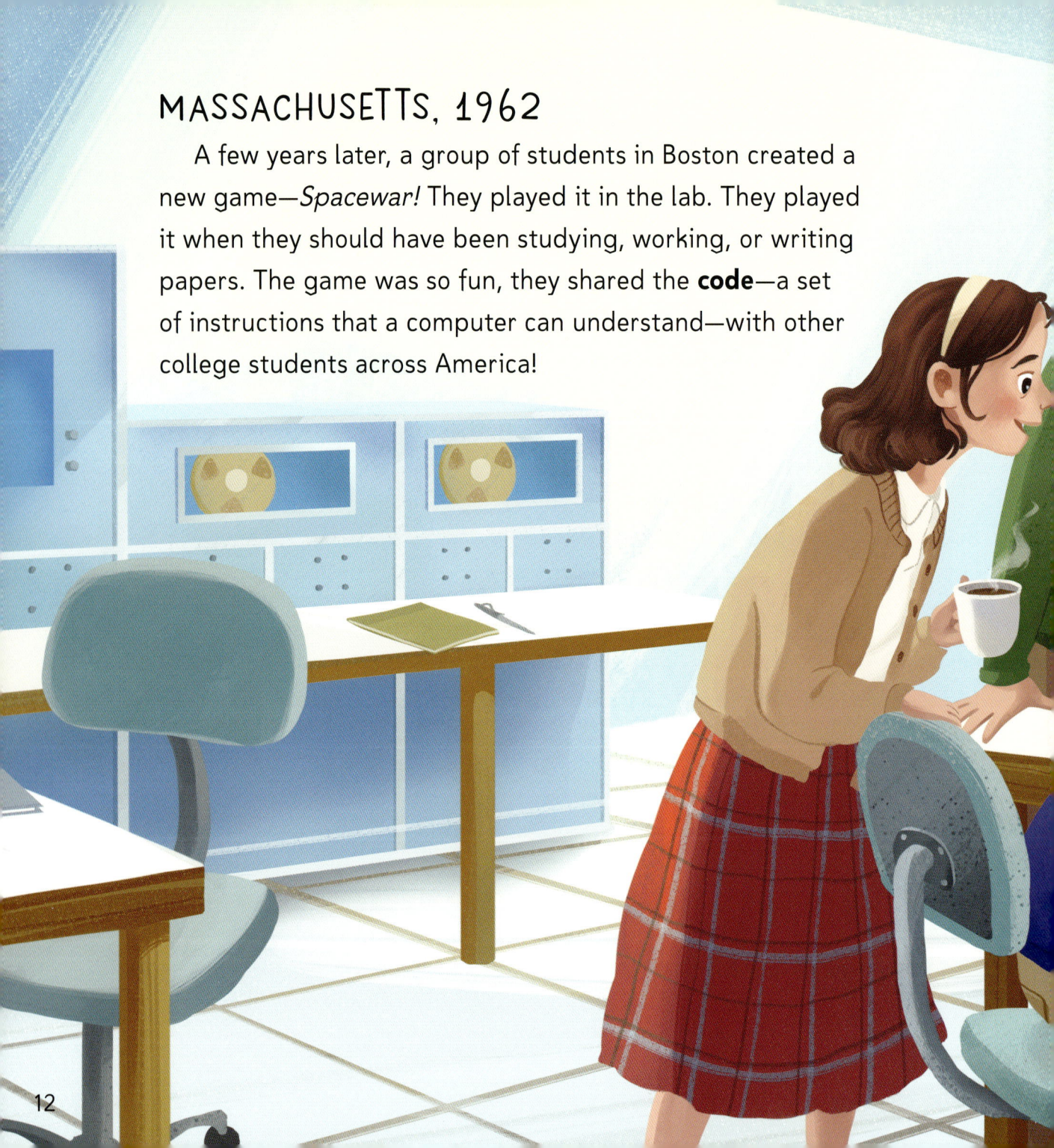

MASSACHUSETTS, 1962

A few years later, a group of students in Boston created a new game—*Spacewar!* They played it in the lab. They played it when they should have been studying, working, or writing papers. The game was so fun, they shared the **code**—a set of instructions that a computer can understand—with other college students across America!

NEW HAMPSHIRE, LATE 1960s

In the 1960s, most people didn't have access to computers. But millions of Americans had televisions for their homes. Ralph H. Baer thought a TV could be used for more than just watching shows. He wanted people to play games on them.

Baer collected spare parts at the company where he worked to build a special box. It sent electrical signals and pictures to a TV screen. Players moved switches on a circuit board to change games.

It was the world's first video game **console**, a small computer used for playing games. His team called it the *Brown Box*.

HOW VIDEO GAMES WORK!

Video games are made up of **hardware** and **software**.

Hardware is the physical parts that make up a video game console.

Software is the game program and information used to run the game.

Coding is the process of writing a computer program using a computer language.

Video game **programmers** use coding to write instructions for the **central processing unit** or CPU.

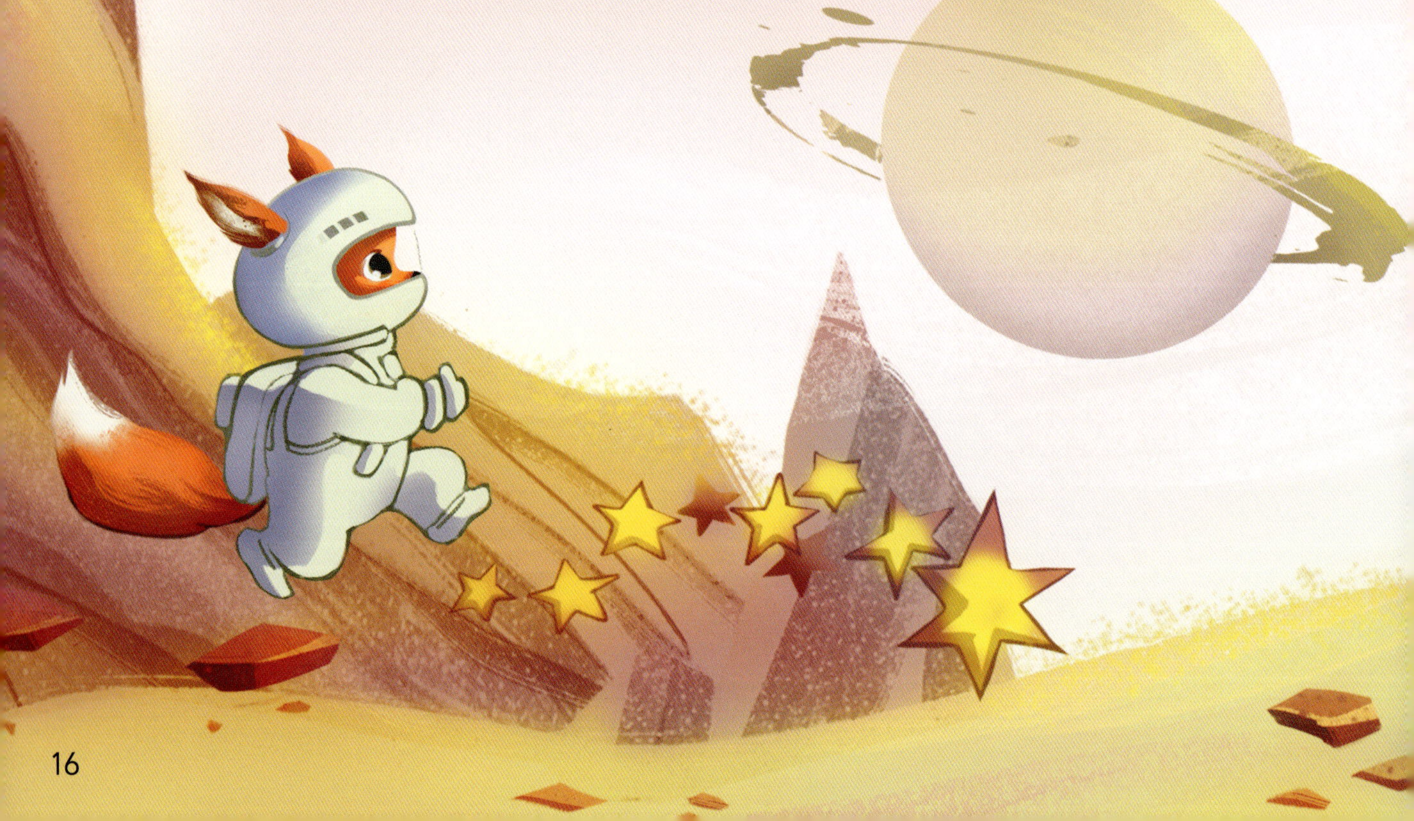

HARDWARE

screen
displays the images

console
a small computer used
for playing games

controller
controls the object or
character in the game

hard drive
stores a computer's
memory

**central
processing unit**
the computer or CPU

graphics card
printed circuit board
that controls the images
sent to the screen

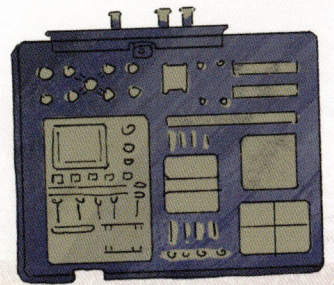

CALIFORNIA, 1970s

Like Baer, Nolan Bushnell wanted to make games for TVs. He started a company called Atari. One of Atari's games was *Pong*. It kept score and made a simple *BLOOP* sound when players hit the ball.

Atari tested *Pong* in a tavern. People came just to play it. Three years later, Bushnell and his team made a small *Pong* game box. It sold well at first, but players grew bored of its only game. *Pong* game boxes ended up in storage closets and garage sales.

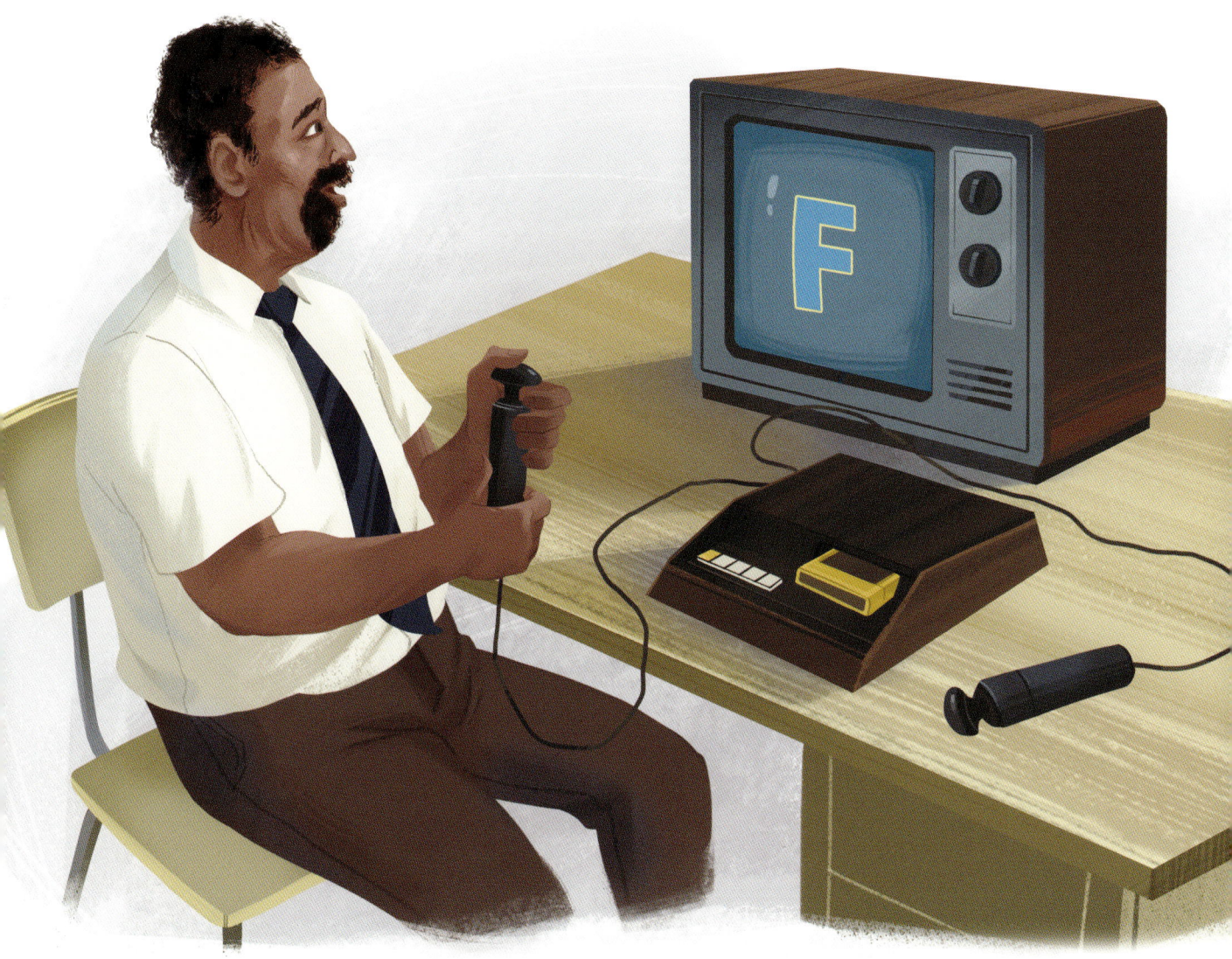

Over at the Fairchild Company, Jerry Lawson was working on a fix for that boredom. His team developed the Channel F system. The *F* stood for "fun." Each game had its own cartridge. Lawson also made a joystick with a pause button. Players could now switch games and take breaks.

JAPAN, 1980

In the 1970s, video games were mostly played in arcades, and arcades were mostly for teens and adults. But then Toru Iwatani created a game that would change the market.

He said he got the idea while grabbing a slice of pizza. Why not make a game about eating? When he looked at the rest of his pizza, he saw his main character—a simple yellow circle with a missing wedge.

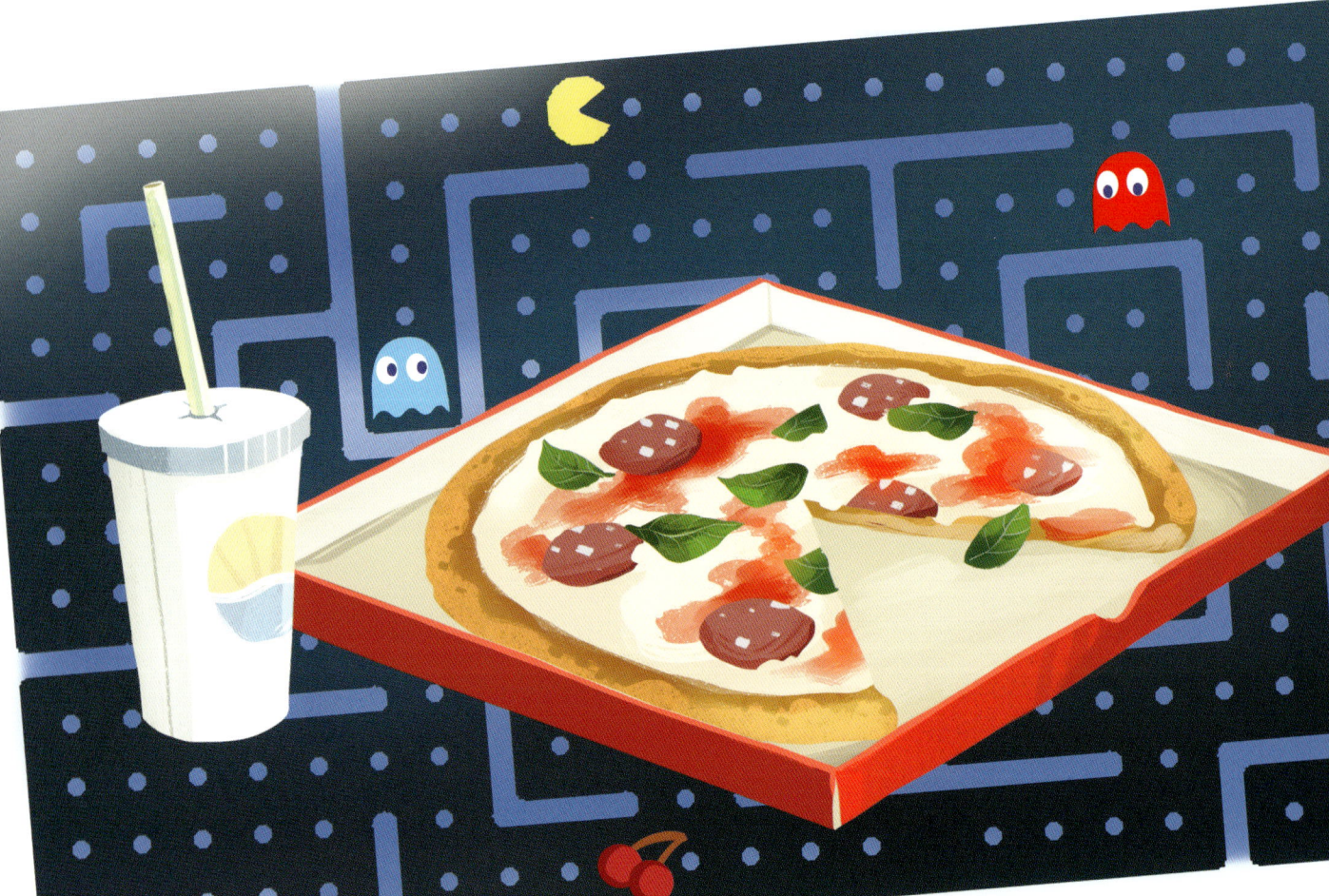

Pac-Man ate his way to the top of the arcade kingdom. Arcades bought rows of machines. Other game designers began to put characters in their games.

Arcade games were on the rise and home video game companies wanted the same success. They rushed to put out new games, too. With so many choices, games became cheaper. The companies that made them weren't making money. Some players grew tired of the low-quality games.

Lots of companies in the United States shut down.
Was it GAME OVER for the industry?

JAPAN, 1983

Not yet! Home video games got an extra boost when Masayuki Uemura designed a different kind of console. The games had more colors. They moved faster. The joystick was gone. Instead games came with a simple controller.

Nintendo brought video gaming back to life!

LATE 1980s

Sega Genesis grew into Nintendo's big rival. *Sonic the Hedgehog* looked as good as an arcade game. Over the next few decades, video games got more and more creative.

1990s

Nintendo came back with *Mario Kart*, which had two players racing against each other on a split screen. And in *Mario Party*, four players could play at the same time!

2000s

Soon, Microsoft's Xbox and Sony's PlayStation 2 hit the scene. PlayStation 2's advanced 3-D graphics made it the bestselling video game console of all time.

Online gaming picked up speed, too. Gamers from around the world could join the same game at the same time.

2010s

With cell phones, games could be played anywhere, any time, and with anyone. Games such as *Pokémon GO* and *Candy Crush* could instantly be downloaded as an app.

Home gaming systems started coming with wireless controllers. Players controlled game characters by moving their own bodies!

Hybrid gaming let players switch from a TV to playing on the go. Before then, players used either handheld consoles or a home system. The Nintendo Switch was both!

2020s

The Oculus Quest transported players to a virtual reality. To them, it felt as if they were *inside* the game!

Video games have come a long way from just a dot and a line on a screen.

They continue to LEVEL UP!

So whether it's at home, on the phone, or over the internet, grab a friend and . . .

get your GAME ON!

••• VIDEO GAME FLASH FACTS •••

• In 1993, *Sonic the Hedgehog* became the first video game character to have a balloon in the Macy's Thanksgiving Day Parade.

• Before video games, Nintendo made and sold playing cards with hand-drawn pictures. The company was founded in 1889!

• Shigeru Miyamoto is one of the most famous game designers in the world. He created many of Nintendo's main characters, including Mario and Luigi, Donkey Kong, and Zelda.

- The first game played in space was *Tetris*. A Russian astronaut packed a handheld Nintendo Game Boy on his mission.

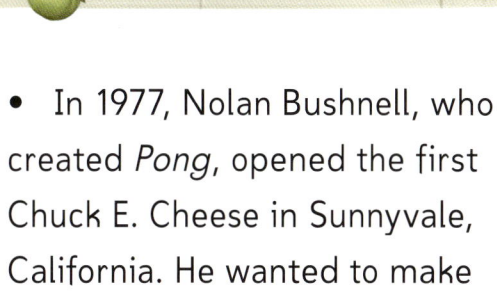

- In 1977, Nolan Bushnell, who created *Pong*, opened the first Chuck E. Cheese in Sunnyvale, California. He wanted to make arcades more kid-friendly.

CANDY LAND

- Many classic board games have gone digital. Gamers can play Monopoly, Scrabble, and Candy Land online.

••• HOW TO MAKE A VIDEO GAME! •••

Video game designers create the GAME PLAN
for how a game will run.

- Rules = How the game should be played
- Space = How the game should look
- Components = Characters, enemies, levels
- Mechanics = Actions, like running and jumping
- Goals = How does the game end?